Anel Cazares (handwritten)

D0517904

Essential Words

Activity Book

MATH

TITLE 1

NEW LEAF

New Leaf Education

www.newleafeducation.com

New Leaf Education has a special offer on new products
for people on our mailing list.
Go to www.newleafeducation.com to learn more.

Design and Cover Illustration:
Ophelia M. Chambliss
Oliver Bliss Design

Printed in the United States of America

10 9 8 7 6 5 4 3 2 1

CoNteNtS

NEW LEAF

Welcome!

To the 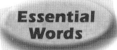 MATH

Activity Book!

About this Book

Here you will find activities to help you learn each term in the Math Glossary. There are more than 200 words to practice while learning and having fun!

Activity Sheets include:

Word Bar with the terms

Different kinds of activities to help with understanding

Page numbers to help you find Essential Words in the Glossary

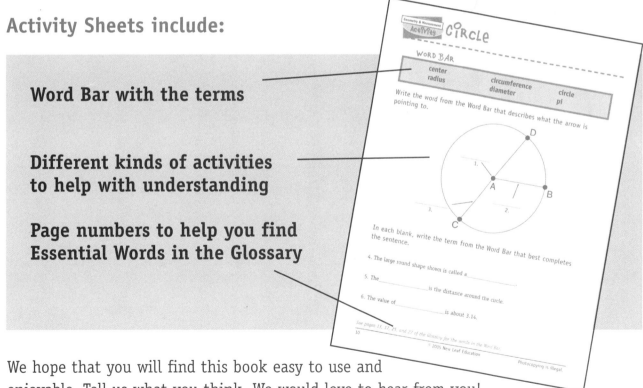

We hope that you will find this book easy to use and enjoyable. Tell us what you think. We would love to hear from you!

www.newleafeducation.com

GRAPHS, PLOTS, AND DIAGRAMS

WORD BAR

bar graph	**circle graph**	**line graph**
line plot	**scatter plot**	**stem-and-leaf plot**
Venn diagram		

Write the name of the graph or plot shown in each figure. Use the words in the Word Bar.

1.

Points in a Game

1	67
2	488
3	0
4	12

2|4 = 24 points

_____

2. Class Grades

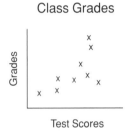

Test Scores

_____

3. Favorite Sport

_____

4. Favorite Music

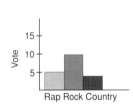

_____

5. Sports Teams

_____

6. People in the Family

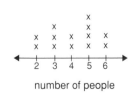

number of people

_____

7. Plant Growth

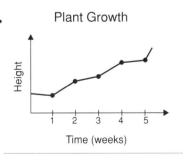

Time (weeks)

_____

See pages 1, 4, 5, 9, and 10 of the Glossary for the words in the Word Bar.

MEAN, MEDIAN, AND OTHERS

WORD BAR

mean	**median**	**mode**	**lower quartile**
range		**upper quartile**	**outlier**

Complete each sentence about the numbers below.

1, 2, 2, 4, 6, 8, 19

1. The mean is _____.

2. The median is _____.

3. The range is _____.

4. The upper quartile is _____.

5. The mode is _____.

6. The lower quartile is _____.

7. The outlier is _____.

See pages 5, 6, 7, 8, and 10 of the Glossary for the words in the Word Bar.

POPULATION AND SAMPLES

WORD BAR

population	bias sample
random sample	sample

For 1-3, one phrase describes the population, and the other phrase describes a sample of that population. Read each description and then check the correct box.

		Population	Sample
1.	a) All the baseball players in the country	☐	☐
	b) All the baseball players in your state	☐	☐
2.	a) The ages of teachers in your school	☐	☐
	b) The ages of teachers in the world	☐	☐
3.	a) All the parks in the city	☐	☐
	b) All the parks near your house	☐	☐

Read each survey question. For each question, tell if the method results in a random sample or bias sample.

	Random Sample	Bias Sample
4. Survey Question: What type of music do students in a school listen to?		
a) Survey students in the school who play classical music.	☐	☐
b) Survey every fifth student in the school.	☐	☐
5. Survey Question: What is your favorite sport?		
a) Ask baseball players.	☐	☐
b) Ask people in your neighborhood.	☐	☐

See pages 1, 8, and 9 of the Glossary for the words in the Word Bar.

FREQUENCY TABLES AND HISTOGRAMS

WORD BAR

data	frequency table	histogram

Match the word with its diagram.

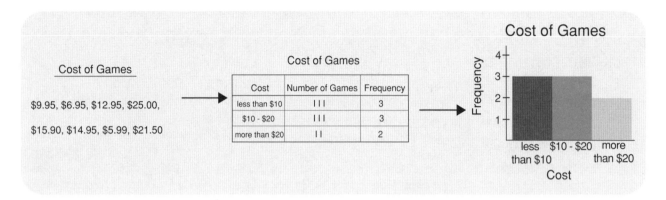

1. data

a)

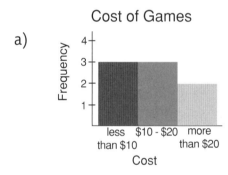

2. frequency table

b)

Cost of Games

Cost	Number of Games	Frequency
less than $10	I I I	3
$10 - $20	I I I	3
more than $20	I I	2

3. histogram

c)

Cost of Games

$9.95, $6.95, $12.95, $25.00,

$15.90, $14.95, $5.99, $21.50

See pages 2-4 of the Glossary for the words in the Word Bar.

PROBABILITY

WORD BAR

dependent event	**event**	**experimental probability**
independent event	**outcome**	**probability**

Choose the word from the Word Bar that best describes each sentence.

Experiment: Pick a shape without looking.

1. The_____of picking the ▲ is $\frac{1}{4}$.

2. The_____(s) are: ●, ■, ▬, ▲ .

3. The ● is one_____or outcome of the experiment.

4. Rick picked a shape 10 times, recorded the result, and put the shape back in the bag each time. He used his results to find the probability of picking a circle. Rick found the_____of picking a circle.

Shape	Number of times picked	
●	I I	2
▬	I I I	3
■	I I I	3
▲	I I	2

Probability of picking a circle: $\frac{2}{10}$

Event 1: picked ■
put ■ back

Event 1 : picked ■
do not put ■ back

Event 2: picked ▲

Event 2: picked ▲

5. Event 2 is a(n)_____.

6. Event 2 is a(n)_____.

See pages 2-4, 7, and 8 of the Glossary for the words in the Word Bar.

COMBINATIONS AND PERMUTATIONS

WORD BAR

combination	permutation
set	tree diagram

For 1-4, check the box to show whether a combination or permutation is described.

Sue , Juan , Lee

	Combination	Permutation
1. You choose some things where order matters.	☐	☐
2. You choose some things where order does not matter.	☐	☐
3. Choose 2 people to join the team:	☐	☐

Team   Sue   Juan   Team   Sue   Lee   Team   Juan   Lee

4. Choose 2 people to be first place and second place: ☐   ☐

1st Sue   2nd Juan   1st Juan   2nd Sue   1st Sue   2nd Lee

1st Lee   2nd Sue   1st Juan   2nd Lee   1st Lee   2nd Juan

Write the term *set* or *tree diagram* under its figure.

5.

Sue — Juan, Lee
Juan — Sue, Lee
Lee — Sue, Juan

_____

6.

Sue , Juan , Lee

_____

See pages 2, 7, 9, and 10 of the Glossary for the words in the Word Bar.

BASIC GEOMETRIC TERMS

WORD BAR

point	line	line segment
plane	ray	congruent

Write the name of the figure using the word from the Word Bar that best describes it.

1.

_____

2.

_____

3.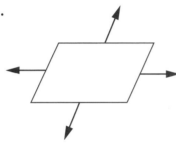

_____

4.

_____

5.

_____

6. Draw a line segment that is congruent to the one shown above.

See pages 15, 20, 21, 25, and 28 of the Glossary for the words in the Word Bar.

INTERSECTING LINES AND ANGLES

WORD BAR

skew lines	parallel lines	perpendicular lines
intersecting lines	vertical angles	corresponding angles
congruent		

Write the name of the figure using the word from the Word Bar that best describes it.

1.

_____

2.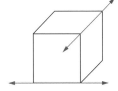

_____

3.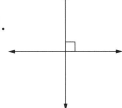

_____

Write the term from the Word Bar that best completes each sentence.

4. ∠ SPQ and ∠ RPT are_____.

5. Lines that cross at a point are called_____.

For 6 and 7, use the figure below.

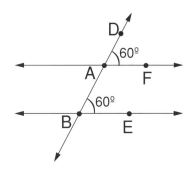

6. ∠ DAF and ∠ DBE are_____.

7. ∠ DAF and ∠ DBE are also_____ because they have the same measure.

See pages 15, 16, 19, 23, 24, 32, and 35 of the Glossary for the words in the Word Bar.

ANGLES

WORD BAR

adjacent angles	angles	acute angle
complementary angles	degrees	obtuse angle
right angle	supplementary angles	
straight angle	vertex	

In each blank, write the word from the Word Bar that describes what type of angle is shown.

1.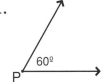

2.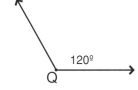

3.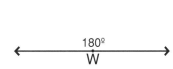

4.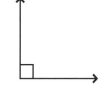

_____ _____ _____ _____

Write the term from the Word Bar that best completes each sentence.

5. The figures shown above, formed by two rays that have the same endpoint, are called _____.

6. ∠ P and ∠ Q are _____. The measurement of their angles adds up to 180º.

7. ∠ W measures 180_____.

8. An angle with a measure of 30º and an angle with a measure of 60º are _____ because they add to 90º.

9. Point S is the_____of ∠ RSU.

10. ∠ RST and ∠ TSU are_____because they share a common vertex and side.

See pages 11-35 of the Glossary for the words in the Word Bar.

WORD BAR

center	circumference	circle
radius	diameter	pi

Write the word from the Word Bar that describes what the arrow is pointing to.

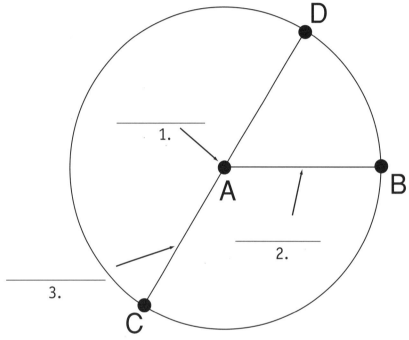

In each blank, write the term from the Word Bar that best completes the sentence.

4. The large round shape shown is called a_____.

5. The_____is the distance around the circle.

6. The value of_____is about 3.14.

See pages 13, 17, 25, and 27 of the Glossary for the words in the Word Bar.

TRIANGLES

WORD BAR

isosceles triangle	**obtuse triangle**	**triangle**
acute triangle	**equilateral triangle**	**right triangle**
scalene triangle	**vertex**	

Name each triangle type. Choose from: acute triangle, right triangle, or obtuse triangle.

1.
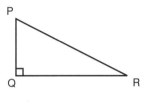

_____

2.

_____

3.
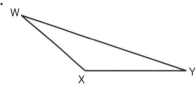

_____

Name each triangle type. Choose from: scalene triangle, isosceles triangle, or equilateral triangle.

4.
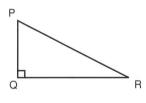

_____

5.

_____

6.
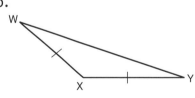

_____

Write the term from the Word Bar that best completes the sentence.

7. The figures shown above are called_____(s) because they have three sides.

8. Point R is called a_____ of △ PRQ.

See pages 11, 18, 20, 22, 30, 31, and 35 of the Glossary for the words in the Word Bar.

QUADRILATERALS

WORD BAR

parallelogram	rectangle	quadrilateral
square	trapezoid	rhombus

Write the name of the figure using the word from the Word Bar that best describes it.

1.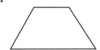

_____

2.

_____

3.

_____

4.

_____

5.

_____

6.

_____

See pages 23, 27-29, 32, and 34 of the Glossary for the words in the Word Bar.

POLYGONS

WORD BAR

pentagon	polygon	regular polygon
hexagon	octagon	

Write the name of the figure using the word from the Word Bar that best describes it.

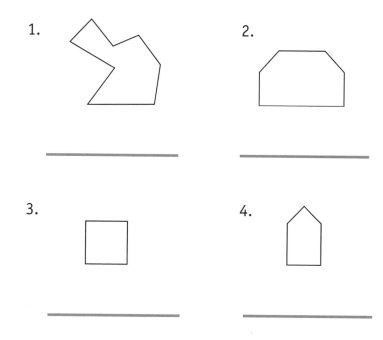

1.

2.

_____

_____

3.

4.

_____

_____

Write the term from the Word Bar that best completes the sentence.

5. The figures shown above are all_____(s). They are closed figures formed by line segments that do not cross.

See pages 18, 23-25, and 29 of the Glossary for the words in the Word Bar.

WORD BAR

similar figures	corresponding angles
scale factor	congruent

In each blank, write the word from the Word Bar that best completes each sentence.

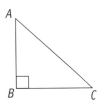

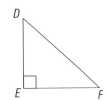

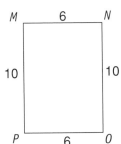

1. △ ABC and △ DEF are_____ △ s because they have the same shape and same size.

2. *MNOP* and *GHIJ* are_____. They are the same shape, but not the same size.

3. ∠ A and ∠ D are_____. They are matching angles.

4. The_____of *MNOP* to *GHIJ* is 2:1.

SOLID FIGURES

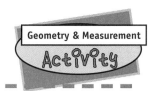

WORD BAR

cone	cube	cylinder
net	pyramid	sphere
polyhedron		

Write the name of the figure using the word from the Word Bar that best describes it.

1.

_____

2.

_____

3.

_____

4.

_____

5.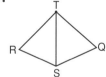

_____

6.

_____

Write the term from the Word Bar that best completes each sentence.

7. The figures shown for #5 and #6 are called_____(s). They are 3-dimensional solids in which all the faces are polygons.

See pages 14, 16, 17, 22, 26, and 32 of the Glossary for the words in the Word Bar.

SOLID FIGURE

WORD BAR

base	edge	face
prism	vertex	

In each blank, write the word from the Word Bar that describes what the arrow is pointing to.

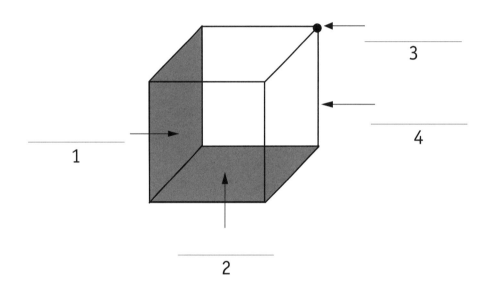

Write the word from the Word Bar that best completes the sentence.

5. The three-dimensional figure shown is called a rectangular_____.

See pages 12, 18, 26, and 35 of the Glossary for the words in the Word Bar.

© 2005 New Leaf Education

Right Triangles

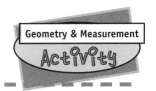
WORD BAR

| legs | right angle | right triangle |
| hypotenuse | Pythagorean theorem | |

In each blank, write the word from the Word Bar that describes what the arrow is pointing to.

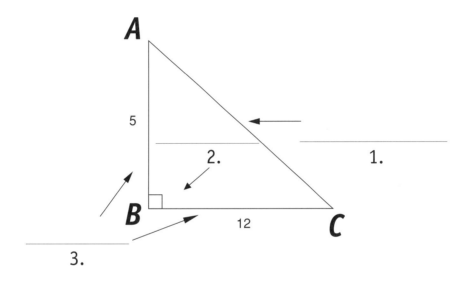

Write the term from the Word Bar that best completes the sentence.

4. The three-sided figure shown with one right angle is also known as a _____.

5. If you want to find the length of $\overline{AC}$, you can use the_____, which states that $(5)^2 + (12)^2 = (\overline{AC})^2$

See pages 19, 20, 27, and 30 of the Glossary for the words in the Word Bar.

TRANSFORMATIONS

WORD BAR

image	line of symmetry	rotation
rotational symmetry	translation	transformation
reflection		

Write the word from the Word Bar that best describes what is shown in the figure.

1.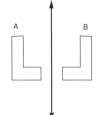

_____

2.

_____

3.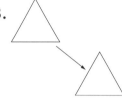

_____

4.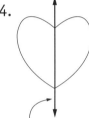

_____

Write the term from the Word Bar that best completes the sentence.

5. Figure B is a(n)_____of figure A.
It is a figure formed by a reflection.

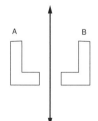

6. This figure has_____because you
can turn it less than 360° around the center and match
the original.

7. The figures in #1, 2, and 3 each show a type of_____.

See pages 19, 21, 28, 30, and 34 of the Glossary for the words in the Word Bar.

PATTERNS

WORD BAR

greatest	least	pattern
sequence	term	

Choose a word from the Word Bar to complete the sentence.

5, 10, 15, 20, 25...

1. The _____ number shown is 5. It is the smallest number.

2. The _____ number shown is 25. It is the largest number.

3. The _____ of this ordered set of numbers is counting by 5s.

4. The set above is an ordered set of numbers. It is also called a _____.

5. The number 10 is one _____ in the pattern.

Complete.

3, 6, 9, 12, 15....

6. Name a term in the sequence. _____

7. What is the pattern? _____

See pages 41, 43, 46, 50, and 52 of the Glossary for the words in the Word Bar.

OPERATIONS

WORD BAR

difference	**sum**	**product**
quotient	**numerical expression**	**order of operations**
divisible	**compatible numbers**	

Match the word that best fits the description.

1. The answer to a division problem. For 6 ÷ 3, it is 2.
           a. product

2. The answer to an addition problem. For 6 + 4, it is 10.
           b. quotient

3. The answer to a subtraction problem. For 8 − 5, it is 3.
           c. sum

4. The answer to a multiplication problem. For 2 × 3, it is 6.
           d. difference

Choose a word from the Word Bar to complete the sentence.

5. To estimate 451 ÷ 49, you can use 450 ÷ 50. The numbers 450 and 50 are
   _____. They are numbers that are easy to calculate with.

6. If 6 ÷ 2 = 3, then we can say that 6 is_____by 2.

7. The expression 5 × 2 + (4 −2) is a_____. It is an expression
   with numbers and one or more operation symbols.

8. For the expression 5 × 2 + (4−2), you perform (4−2) first. This follows the
   _____.

See pages 39, 40, 45, 46, 48, and 51 of the Glossary for the words in the Word Bar.

FACTORS

WORD BAR

common factor	**factor**
factor tree	**greatest common factor**

Choose a word from the Word Bar to complete the sentence.

Factors of 12: 1, 2, 3, 4, 6, 12
Factors of 18: 1, 2, 3, 6, 9, 18

1. A _____ of 18 is 9.

2. The _____(s) of 12 and 18 are 1, 2, 3, and 6.

3. The number 6 is the _____ of 12 and 18.

4. A _____ for 28 looks like this:

```
    28
   / \
  7x 4
  | / \
  7 x 2x2
```

Complete each sentence.

5. The factors of 8 are _____.

6. The common factors of 8 and 12 are _____.

7. The greatest common factor of 8 and 12 is _____.

See pages 38, 41, and 42 of the Glossary for the words in the Word Bar.

PRiMe AND CoMPoSite

WORD BAR

composite numbers   **prime numbers**   **prime factorization** **relatively prime numbers**   **greatest**   **least**

Choose a word from the Word Bar to complete the sentence.

1. The numbers 2, 3, 5, 7, 23, 37 are _____. Each has exactly two factors, 1 and itself.

2. The numbers 8 and 15 are _____. They are not prime, but their greatest common factor is 1.

3. For the number 12, the _____ is 2 × 2 × 3, or 2^2 × 3.

4. The numbers 6, 12, and 15 are _____. Each has more than 2 factors.

5. The_____number in the set {6, 12, 15} is 15.

6. The_____number in the set {6, 12, 15} is 6.

Complete.

7. Write a number that is relatively prime to 14.   _____

8. Write the prime factorization of 48.   _____

9. Circle the prime numbers: 16, 17, 21, 24, 29, 41.

10. Circle the composite numbers: 3, 12, 22, 37, 50, 63.

11. Circle the greatest number: 3, 12, 22, 37, 51, 63.

12. Circle the least number: 3, 12, 22, 37, 51, 63.

See pages 39, 41, 43, 47, and 49 of the Glossary for the words in the Word Bar.

sets of NUMBers

WORD BAR

integers	**natural numbers**	**whole numbers**
real numbers	**irrational numbers**	**rational numbers**
terminating decimal	**repeating decimal**	

Match the words that best describe the set.

1. 0, 1, 2, 3, 4

2. -4, -3, -2, -1, 0, 1, 2, 3, 4

3. 1, 2, 3, 4, 5, 6

4. $\frac{-5}{6}$, 0, 1.2, $\sqrt{2}$, ππ, 18

5. $\frac{-5}{6}$, 0, 1.2, 18

6. $\sqrt{2}$, ππ

a) whole numbers

b) natural numbers

c) integers

d) real numbers

e) irrational numbers

f) rational numbers

Write the word from the Word Bar that best completes each sentence.

7. The decimal 0.33333..... is also known as a _____. The number 3 repeats.

8. The decimal 4.56 is known as a _____. It ends.

See pages 43, 45, 48, 49, and 52 of the Glossary for the words in the Word Bar.

PROPERTIES

WORD BAR

Associative Property of Addition
Associative Property of Multiplication
Commutative Property of Addition
Commutative Property of Multiplication
Identity Property of Zero for Addition
Zero Property of Multiplication
Identity Property of One for Multiplication
Distributive Property

Tell which property from the Word Bar is shown.

Property

1. $(5 + 6) + 4 = 5 + (6 + 4)$ _____

2. $4 \times 0 = 0$ _____

3. $2 \times 3 = 3 \times 2$ _____

4. $5 (4 + 6) = (5 \times 4) + (5 \times 6)$ _____

5. $8 + 0 = 8$ _____

6. $9 + 5 = 5 + 9$ _____

7. $1 \times 8 = 8$ _____

8. $(5 \times 4) \times 7 = 5 \times (4 \times 7)$ _____

See pages 37-39, 42, and 52 of the Glossary for the words in the Word Bar.

ABSolute VALue

WORD BAR

| absolute value | inverse operations | opposite |

Choose a word from the Word Bar to complete the sentence.

1. The _____ of 6 is –6.
   –6 is the same distance from 0 on the number line as 6.

2. The _____ of 6 is 6. The distance of 6 from 0 is 6 units.

3. Addition and subtraction are _____. They undo each other.

Complete.

4. The absolute value of –5 is _____.

5. The opposite of -7 is _____.

6. The inverse operation to division is _____.

See pages 37, 43, and 45 of the Glossary for the words in the Word Bar.

Photocopying is illegal.

RATIO AND PROPORTION

WORD BAR

proportion	**ratio**	**scale model**
equivalent fractions	**cross product**	

Look at the figure below. Write the term from the Word Bar that best completes the sentence.

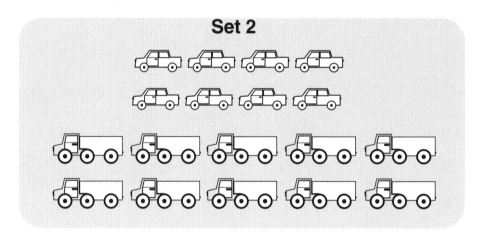

1. In Set 1, the_____of cars to trucks is 4:5; in Set 2 it is 8:10.

2. The truck shown is a_____of an actual truck.

3. The ratios $\frac{4}{5}$ and $\frac{8}{10}$ are_____.

4. The equation $\frac{4}{5} = \frac{8}{10}$ is called a_____.

5. For the equation $\frac{4}{5} = \frac{8}{10}$, 5 × 8 and 4 × 10 are called_____(s).

See pages 53-56 of the Glossary for the words in the Word Bar.

© 2005 New Leaf Education

PERCENT, RATES, AND SCALE

WORD BAR

discount	percent	rate
scale drawing	scale	unit rate

Write the word from the Word Bar that best completes the sentence.

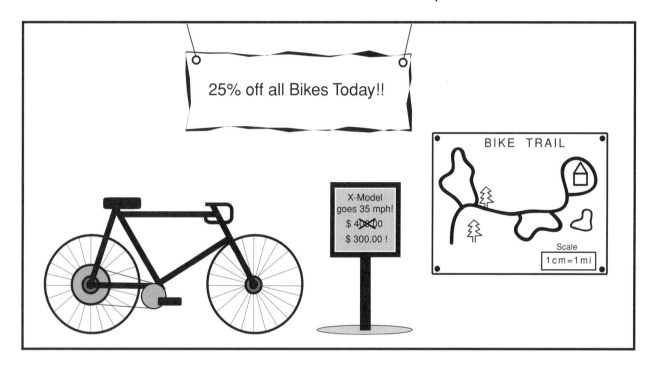

1. Every bike is on sale for 25_____off.

2. The X-model bike has a_____of $100.00.

3. The bike trail map is a_____of the actual bike trail.

4. The_____that the bike can travel is 35 miles per hour.

5. <u>35 miles</u> is also known as a_____.
   1 hour

6. The_____of the map is 1 cm=1 mile.

See pages 53-56 of the Glossary for the words in the Word Bar.

PRINCIPAL AND INTEREST

WORD BAR

principal	interest

Read each description below. Check the box of the term for each description.

	Principal	Interest
1. money that you put in a savings account	☐	☐
2. money that a bank pays you for having your money in a savings account	☐	☐
3. money that you borrow	☐	☐
4. money that you pay a bank, in addition to the amount you borrowed	☐	☐
5. money that you pay, in addition to the cost of the item you bought	☐	☐

See page 54 of the Glossary for the words in the Word Bar.

PROPERTIES of EQUALITY

Equations & Inequalities
Activity

WORD BAR

Addition Property of Equality
Division Property of Equality
Multiplication Property of Equality
Subtraction Property of Equality

Draw lines to match the terms with the examples.

1. Addition Property of Equality

2. Division Property of Equality

3. Multiplication Property of Equality

4. Subtraction Property of Equality

a) $\underline{3 \qquad 3}$ $3 = 3$

$\underline{3 \times 4 \quad 3 \times 4}$ $3 \times 4 = 3 \times 4$

b) $\underline{8 \qquad 8}$ $8 = 8$

$\underline{8 \div 2 \quad 8 \div 2}$ $\dfrac{8}{2} = \dfrac{8}{2}$

c) $\underline{4 \qquad 4}$ $4 = 4$

$\underline{4 - 1 \quad 4 - 1}$ $4 - 1 = 4 - 1$

d) $\underline{6 \qquad 6}$ $6 = 6$

$\underline{x + 6 \quad x + 6}$ $x + 6 = x + 6$

See pages 57 and 59 of the Glossary for the words in the Word Bar.

      Photocopying is illegal.

EQUATIONS AND INEQUALITIES

WORD BAR

equation	formula
inequality	solution

Write the term from the Word Bar that best completes the sentence.

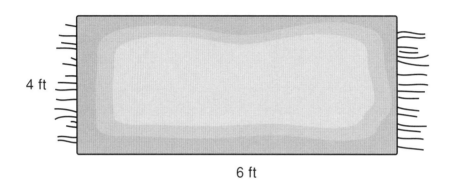

4 ft

6 ft

1. The width *(w)* of the rug is equal to *4ft*, or *w= 4ft*. *w= 4ft* is a(n)_____because it shows two equal quantities.

2. To find the area of the rug, you can use the_____*A= lw* where l is the length of the rug, and *w* is the width of the rug.

3. The_____to *A= 6ft* x *4ft* is *24ft²* .

4. The area of Maggie's room is greater than *24ft²* . If M= area of Maggie's room, you can write a(n)_____*M > 24ft²* .

See pages 58 and 59 of the Glossary for the words in the Word Bar.

VARIABLES AND EXPRESSIONS

WORD BAR

algebraic expression	monomial	polynomial
term variable	binomial	simplify

Circle the best example for each term.

1. variable   A) 3   B) g C) 2(4)+1

2. monomial   A) $3x^2 + y + 2$ B) $3x^2 + 1$ C) $3x^2y$

3. term   A) 6x-<u>7yz</u>+1   B) 6<u>x</u>-7yz+1   C) <u>6x-7yz</u>+1

4. algebraic expression   A) $5abc$ B) - 9   C) $9^2 - 4$

5. binomial   A) $2a + b$ B) $2a + b - 3c$ C) $2a$

6. Give an example of a polynomial.

7. If you _____ 6x – 2x, the answer is 4x.

See pages 60 and 61 of the Glossary for the words in the Word Bar.

Like terms and coefficients

WORD BAR

coefficient	like terms

Circle the term to show like terms.

1. $4x$ (A) $-3x$ B) 4   C) x^2

2. $6a^3b$ A) $6ab$ B) $6a^3$ (C) $\dfrac{1}{2}a^3b$

3. $-xyz$ A) $-xy$ (B) $5xyz$ C) yz

4. $12r^3st^4$ A) $12rst$ B) $5r^4st^3$ (C) $-7r^3st^4$

Circle the coefficients.

5. $\boxed{4}x$ 6. $\boxed{6}a^3b$ 7. $\boxed{12}r^3st^4$

8. $x + 60 = 135$ $\begin{array}{r} 135 \\ -\ 60 \end{array}$ $x = 75$

9. $\dfrac{3x}{3} = \dfrac{45}{3}$ $x = 15$

See page 60 of the Glossary for the words in the Word Bar.

COORDINATE PLANE TERMS

WORD BAR

y-axis	*x*-axis	*y*-intercept
x-intercept	Quadrant II	Quadrant I
origin	*x*-coordinate	*y*-coordinate
Quadrant III	Quadrant IV	

Write the term from the Word Bar that describes what the arrow is pointing to. Quadrant I has been done for you.

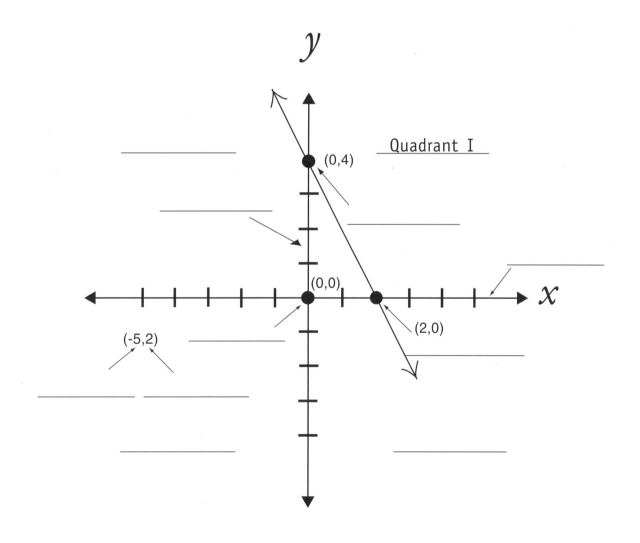

See pages 64, 65, and 67-69 of the Glossary for the words in the Word Bar.

FUNCTION AND SLOPE

WORD BAR

function	ordered pair	coordinate plane
slope	coordinates	

Match the words with the figures.

a)

x	-1	0	1	2
y	-2	0	2	4

1. coordinate plane

b)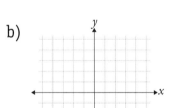

2. function

c)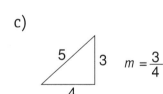

3. slope

Write the term from the Word Bar that best completes the sentence.

4. One of the_____(s) for the table above is (2,4).

5. The_____of the ordered pair (2,4) are 2 and 4.

See pages 62-64 and 66 of the Glossary for the words in the Word Bar.

Linear Function and Slope-Intercept Form

WORD BAR

linear function	slope-intercept form

Check whether the equation is a linear function.

		Yes	No
1.	$y = x^2$	☐	☐

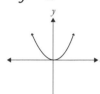

| 2. | $y = 3x$ | ☐ | ☐ |

| 3. | $y = -x + 1$ | ☐ | ☐ |

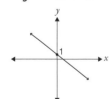

Check whether the equations are in slope–intercept form.

		Yes	No
4.	$y = 2x + 3$	☐	☐
5.	$2y - 3x = 4$	☐	☐
6.	$x = -2y + 5$	☐	☐

See pages 63 and 67 of the Glossary for the words in the Word Bar.

TRANSFORMATIONS

WORD BAR

reflection	translation	rotation

Match the terms with the correct transformation.

1. rotation

a)

2. reflection

b)

3. translation

c)

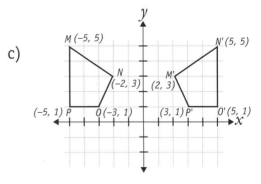

See pages 65-67 of the Glossary for the words in the Word Bar.

© 2005 New Leaf Education